BRITISH RAILWAYS STEAMING ON THE WESTERN REGION

Volume Five

Compiled by
PETER HANDS

DEFIANT PUBLICATIONS
190 Yoxall Road
Shirley, Solihull
West Midlands

Printed on behalf of Richard Netherwood Limited, by Gorenjski tisk p.o. Slovenia.

CURRENT STEAM PHOTOGRAPH ALBUMS AVAILABLE
FROM DEFIANT PUBLICATIONS

BRITISH RAILWAYS STEAMING THROUGH THE SIXTIES

VOLUME 14
A4 size - Hardback. 96 pages
-178 b/w photographs.
£14.95 + £1.50 postage.
ISBN 0 946857 40 7.

BRITISH RAILWAYS STEAMING THROUGH THE SIXTIES

VOLUME 15
A4 size - Hardback. 96 pages
-178 b/w photographs.
£16.95 + £1.50 postage.
ISBN 0 946857 52 0.

BRITISH RAILWAYS STEAMING THROUGH WALES AND THE WELSH BORDER

A4 size - Hardback. 96 pages
-175 b/w photographs.
£17.95 + £1.50 postage.
ISBN 0 946857 56 3.

BRITISH RAILWAYS STEAM HAULED PASSENGER TRAINS IN THE SIXTIES

VOLUME 1
A4 size - Hardback. 96 pages
-177 b/w photographs.
£14.95 + £1.50 postage.
ISBN 0 946857 41 5.

BRITISH RAILWAYS STEAMING IN THE NORTH WEST

IN PREPARATION

BRITISH RAILWAYS STEAMING IN THE SOUTH WEST

IN PREPARATION

BRITISH RAILWAYS STEAMING THROUGH THE FIFTIES

VOLUME 11
A4 size - Hardback. 96 pages
-176 b/w photographs.
£16.95 + £1.50 postage.
ISBN 0 946857 48 2.

BRITISH RAILWAYS STEAMING THROUGH THE FIFTIES

VOLUME 12
A4 size - Hardback. 96 pages
-176 b/w photographs.
£16.95 + £1.50 postage.
ISBN 0 946857 49 0.

BRITISH RAILWAYS STEAM HAULED PASSENGER TRAINS IN THE FIFTIES

VOLUME 1
A4 size - Hardback. 96 pages
-177 b/w photographs.
£14.95 + £1.50 postage.
ISBN 0 946857 39 3.

BRITISH RAILWAYS STEAM HAULED FREIGHT TRAINS 1948-1968

VOLUME 1
A4 size - Hardback. 96 pages
-174 b/w photographs.
£14.95 + £1.50 postage.
ISBN 0 946857 42 3.

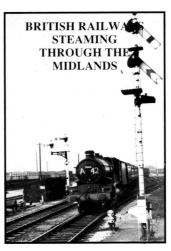

BRITISH RAILWAYS STEAMING THROUGH THE MIDLANDS

VOLUME 1
A4 size - Hardback. 96 pages
-179 b/w photographs.
£15.95 + £1.50 postage.
ISBN 0 946857 43 I.

BRITISH RAILWAYS STEAMING THROUGH THE SIXTIES

IN PREPARATION

VOLUME 16

FUTURE STEAM PHOTOGRAPH ALBUMS
AND OTHER TITLES

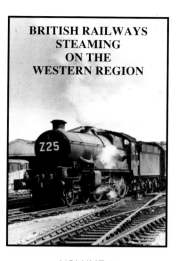

BRITISH RAILWAYS STEAMING ON THE WESTERN REGION

VOLUME 4
A4 size - Hardback. 96 pages
-177 b/w photographs.
£15.95 + £1.50 postage.
ISBN 0 946857 46 6.

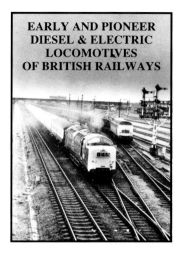

EARLY AND PIONEER DIESEL & ELECTRIC LOCOMOTIVES OF BRITISH RAILWAYS

A4 size - Hardback. 96 pages
-177 b/w photographs.
£15.95 + £1.50 postage.
ISBN 0 946857 45 8.

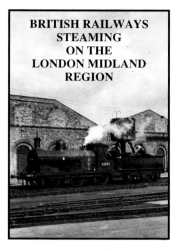

BRITISH RAILWAYS STEAMING ON THE LONDON MIDLAND REGION

VOLUME 4
A4 size - Hardback. 96 pages
-177 b/w photographs.
£15.95 + £1.50 postage.
ISBN 0 946857 47 4.

BRITISH RAILWAYS STEAMING ON THE SOUTHERN REGION

VOLUME 3
A4 size - Hardback. 96 pages
-177 b/w photographs.
£17.95 + £1.50 postage.
ISBN 0 946857 54 7.

BRITISH RAILWAYS STEAM HAULED TITLED TRAINS

A4 size - Hardback. 96 pages
-169 b/w photographs.
£16.95 + £1.50 postage.
ISBN 0 946857 51 2.

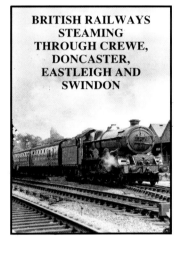

BRITISH RAILWAYS STEAMING THROUGH CREWE, DONCASTER, EASTLEIGH AND SWINDON

A4 size - Hardback. 96 pages
-179 b/w photographs.
£17.95 + £1.50 postage.
ISBN 0 946857 53 9.

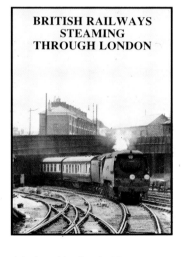

BRITISH RAILWAYS STEAMING THROUGH LONDON

A4 size - Hardback. 96 pages
-174 b/w photographs.
£17.95 + £1.50 postage.
ISBN 0 946857 55 5.

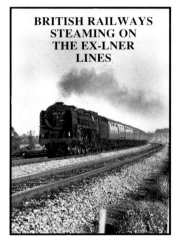

BRITISH RAILWAYS STEAMING ON THE EX-LNER LINES

VOLUME 4
A4 size - Hardback. 96 pages
-183 b/w photographs.
£17.95 + £1.50 postage.
ISBN 0 946857 57 1.

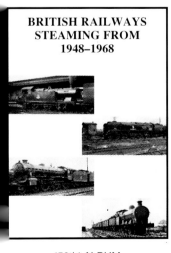

BRITISH RAILWAYS STEAMING FROM 1948–1968

'50th' ALBUM
A4 size - Hardback. 96 pages
-186 b/w photographs.
£16.95 + £1.50 postage.
SBN 0 946857 50 4.

BRITISH RAILWAYS STEAMING ON THE LONDON MIDLAND REGION

VOLUME 5
A4 size - Hardback. 96 pages.
- 177 b/w photographs.
£17.95 + £1.50 postage.
ISBN 0 946857 58X.

BRITISH RAILWAYS STEAMING ON THE WESTERN REGION

VOLUME 5
A4 size - Hardback. 96 pages.
- 177 b/w photographs.
£17.95 + £1.50 postage.
ISBN 0 946857 59 8.

It's a dog's life in the FIRE SERVICE
by Peter St.Bernard

COMEDY
269 pages. Cartoons.
£9.95 + £1.00 postage.
ISBN 0 946857 30 X.

ACKNOWLEDGEMENTS

Grateful thanks are extended to the following contributors of photographs not only for their use in this book but for their kind patience and long term loan of negatives/photographs whilst this book was being compiled.

T.R.AMOS TAMWORTH	P.A.BRIDGMAN HUCCLECOTE	N.L.BROWNE ALDERSHOT
R.S.CARPENTER BIRMINGHAM	TIM FAREBROTHER BOURTON	J.M.GARDINER BIRMINGHAM
A.N.H.GLOVER BIRMINGHAM	B.K.B.GREEN WARRINGTON	PETER HAY HOVE
R.W.HINTON GLOUCESTER	I.J.HODSON CAMBRIDGE	F.HORNBY NORTH CHEAM
L.C.JACKS BIRMINGHAM	D.K.JONES MOUNTAIN ASH	T.LEWIS *
ERIC LIGHT TICKHILL	S.L.C.PHILIPS LLANDYSSUL	R.PICTON WOLVERHAMPTON
W.POTTER BISHOPS CLEEVE	N.E.PREEDY GLOUCESTER	P.A.ROWLINGS ALCONBURY
J.SCHATZ LITTLETHORPE	M.S.STOKES MARPLE	G.H.TRURAN GLASTONBURY
A.WAKEFIELD DRONFIELD	M.WOOD BIRMINGHAM	

* Courtesy of the Norman Preedy collection.

Front Cover - GWR *Hall* Class 4-6-0 No 5910 *Park Hall*, from 82A Bristol (Bath Road), makes a spirited start to its eastbound journey as it leaves Penzance with an up van train on 20th August 1956. In February 1959 *Park Hall* was transferred to 86C Cardiff (Canton) where it remained until being drafted to a final abode at 84B Oxley (Wolverhampton) from whence it was withdrawn in September 1962, (N.L.Browne)

ISBN 0 946857 59 8

(C) P.B.HANDS 1997
FIRST PUBLISHED 1997

INTRODUCTION

BRITISH RAILWAYS STEAMING ON THE WESTERN REGION - Volume 5 is the fifth book to concentrate on the Western Region of British Railways. This fifth album contains a wide and varied selection of photographs provided by some twenty-seven contributors of steam at work and rest from in excess of ninety different locations on the Western Region from the late 1940's until the end of 1965 when most of the allocated steam on the region ceased. Some areas of greater interest, such as Birmingham, Bristol, Gloucester, Oxford, Reading and Swindon have been given more coverage than others.

These books are designed to give the ordinary, everyday steam photographic enthusiast of the 1950's and 1960's a chance to participate in and give pleasure to others whilst recapturing the twilight days of steam.

Apart from the main 1950's and 1960's series, further individual albums like this one will be produced from time to time. Wherever possible, no famous names will be found nor will photographs which have been published before be used. Nevertheless, the content and quality of the majority of photographs selected will be second to none.

The majority of the photographs used in this album have been contributed by readers of Peter Hands series of booklets entitled "What Happened to Steam" and "BR Steam Shed Allocations" (both still available) and from readers of the earlier "BR Steaming Through The Sixties" albums. Under normal circumstances these may have been hidden from the public eye for ever.

The continuation of the "BR Steaming" series etc., depends upon you the reader. If you wish to join my mailing list for future albums and/or feel you have suitable material of BR steam locomotives between 1948-1968 and wish to contribute them towards this series and other albums, please contact:-

Tel No.
0121 745-8421

Peter Hands,
190 Yoxall Road,
Shirley, Solihull,
West Midlands B90 3RN

BEST WISHES

Peter Hands

CONTENTS

Memories of the Western Region of British Railways

1) Kingham station facing Worcester - circa 1961. (R.S.Carpenter)

2) Bampton station in Devon in June 1961. (N.L.Browne)

3) Broadway station in 1958. (R.S.Carpenter)

4) 82G Templecombe shed on 20th October 1962. (J.Schatz)

5) Tetbury sub-shed on 19th October 1963. (J.Schatz)

6) Sunlight and shadow within the confines of number five shed at 84A Wolverhampton (Stafford Road) on 31st August 1960 where GWR *King* Class 4-6-0 No 6014 *King Henry VII*, a locally based steed, is being prepared for its next passenger duty to Paddington. Constructed at Swindon in May 1928, *King Henry VII* retained the 'wedge-fronted' cab from its streamlined days right up until withdrawal from Stafford Road in September 1962. (M.S.Stokes)

7) With the back end of the local shed in the left of the frame, GWR *Castle* Class 4-6-0 No 5076 *Gladiator*, from 81A Old Oak Common, steams beneath a signal gantry and enters Oxford station with a Worcester to Paddington express in December 1963. *Gladiator*, another product of Swindon Works, is in the twilight of its career with less than twelve months to live. It was condemned from 81C Southall in September 1964. (I.J.Hodson)

8) With a GWR 4-6-0 type lurking in the background the focus of the photographer's attention is on GWR Collett 5101 Class 2-6-2T No 5156 seen in the shed yard at 84E Tyseley on a grey looking 22nd May 1949. No 5156 worked on local passenger and freight trains in the Birmingham area until October 1957, when it was transferred to 85C Hereford. In May 1958 it was briefly based at 85A Worcester before returning to 85C prior to withdrawal later in the year. (A.N.H.Glover)

9) Another Tyseley locomotive (looking brand new) heads southwards light engine on a through track at Birmingham (Snow Hill) station on a sunny 26th July 1952. During its brief career BR Class 3 2-6-2T No 82001 worked from a host of other depots, including 88F Treherbert, 82A Bristol (Bath Road), 6E Chester (GWR), 6A Chester (LMR), 82G Templecombe, 86C Cardiff (Canton), 72A Exmouth Junction, 83B Taunton, 82E Bristol Barrow Road and 82F Bath Green Park. (N.E.Preedy)

10) 83D Laira (Plymouth) allocated GWR *Grange* Class 4-6-0 No 6848 *Toddington Grange* is noted at Newton Abbot station during the early part of 1957 in charge of a local passenger working to Kingswear shortly before being transferred to 84C Banbury. During the latter stages of its working life *Toddington Grange* spent a number of years based at 86G Pontypool Road. Condemnation for No 6848 came from 85A Worcester in December 1965. (D.K.Jones)

11) For many years the popular GWR *Manor* Class 4-6-0's made the former Cambrian Railways lines their own and they were often employed on the famous *Cambrian Coast Express*. Sporting the headboard of the same, No 7810 *Draycott Manor*, of 89D Oswestry, has steam to spare next to the water tank in the yard at Aberystwyth shed in July 1963. Although many examples are preserved today, No 7810 is not one of them, being cut up in 1965. (R.W.Hinton)

12) With the 'factory' in the background and with a 'keen-looking' member of the railway fraternity in the left foreground, Hawksworth inspired GWR 1600 Class 0-6-0PT No 1648, of 87C Danygraig, looks fresh from shops in the yard at Swindon Works on 24th June 1951. No 1648 remained at Danygraig shed until it closed to steam in January 1960, moving to a new abode at 87G Carmarthen. Withdrawal came from 87H Neyland in May 1963. (B.K.B.Green)

13) An 'unusual' gantry of lower quadrant signals towers over GWR *Manor* Class 4-6-0 No 7817 *Garsington Manor*, based locally at 81D, as it stands in Reading station on 1st June 1963. Once of 84J Croes Newydd (twice), 84G Shrewsbury and 84F Stourbridge, *Garsington Manor* had been at Reading shed since September 1962. Withdrawn from 81D in June 1964 it was stored there for several months before being despatched to South Wales for scrapping. (D.K.Jones)

14) LMS Ivatt 'Flying Pig' Class 4 2-6-0 No 43049, from 21A Saltley, poses for the camera next to the running shed at 85A Worcester in 1962. Introduced in 1947 a number of the class were allocated to Saltley and were used on local services, particularly to Malvern Wells where they were regular visitors on the morning and evening service from Birmingham (New Street) until ousted by diesel traction in the mid-sixties. (Tim Farebrother)

5) With Temple Meads station in the background, GWR 4300 Class 2-6-0 No 6352 gently lifts its safety valves as it rests in the yard at 82A Bristol (Temple Meads) in the company of a GWR 5700 Class 0-6-0PT on 8th May 1955. Looking ex.works No 6352 is a visitor to 82A from 86C Cardiff (Canton) a depot it was to remain at until taken out of revenue earning service in November 1960. After a brief period of storage it was scrapped at Swindon. (B.K.B.Green)

6) Allocated to 83A Newton Abbot, GWR 2800 Class 2-8-0 No 3834 passes Highbridge Crossing signalbox with a down van train and rattles over the former Somerset and Dorset Joint Railway line from Highbridge to Burnham-on-Sea on 13th September 1958. Ousted from 83A in November 1959, No 3834 was drafted to South Wales at 87F Llanelly. It later served at 86E Severn Tunnel Junction, 81C Southall and 83B Taunton. (N.L.Browne)

17) With only four months left to live, 41A Darnall (Sheffield) based LMS *Royal Scot* Class 4-6-0 No 46151 *The Royal Horse Guardsman* descends the infamous Lickey incline with the 10.10am Newcastle to Cardiff express on 25th August 1962. Once of 5A Crewe (North) and 9A Longsight (Manchester), No 46151 had been drafted to the Eastern Region at 41C Millhouses in February 1960. After withdrawal in December 1962 it was scrapped at Crewe Works. (R.Picton)

18) A once longstanding resident of 85A Worcester, BR Class 2 2-6-0 No 78009 was reallocated to the former Midland Railway depot at 85C Gloucester (Barnwood) in March 1962 where it is seen near to weed-strewn tracks in the shed yard on 11th June 1963. Although looking in fine external condition it was rendered surplus to operating requirements in February 1964 and condemned. Scrapping came in December 1964 at Swindon Works. (D.K.Jones)

9) More weed-strewn and neglected trackwork, this time at the rear of 81E Didcot on 24th June 1951. Standing out of steam in isolation is locally based 2251 Class 0-6-0 No 3212. Records show us that this locomotive was still at Didcot shed until July 1959 when it moved to a new abode at 82D Westbury. It then went to 87J Goodwick in May 1960 but returned to 82D four months later. Its final home was at 86E Severn Tunnel Junction. (B.K.B.Green)

20) In steam days during the summer months Aller Junction was an extremely busy place and a constant stream of trains were the order of the day. During the summer of 1959 GWR *Modified Hall* Class 4-6-0 No 6993 *Arthog Hall*, of 82C Swindon, is employed on a local passenger working. Note the semaphore signals in the background which were only replaced by colour lights in more recent times. The end for No 6993 came in December 1965. (Eric Light)

21) Sporting a local passenger headcode a fully coaled GWR *Grange* Class 4-6-0 No 6858 *Woolston Grange* is a visitor to 81D Reading from 2B Oxley (Wolverhampton) on 20th June 1964. During the late fifties and up until condemnation in October 1965, No 6858 worked from a host of sheds apart from Oxley - 83D Laira (Plymouth), 81F Oxford, 83G Penzance, 86C Cardiff (Canton), 84G Shrewsbury and 84E/2A Tyseley (twice). It was cut up at Cohens, Kingsbury. (D.K.Jones)

22) Looking in reasonable external condition GWR *Hall* Class 4-6-0 No 4907 *Broughton Hall*, of 81C Southall, takes on water supplies in the shed yard at 84F Stourbridge on 23rd August 1958. No 4907 takes its name from the Hall which is far from Western Region territory in Skipton, North Yorkshire. No 4907 moved from 81C Southall to 85A Worcester in November 1959. Its last home was at 86C Hereford from whence it was condemned in August 1963. (N.E.Preedy)

3) With steam to spare begrimed mixed traffic LMS Class 6P5F 2-6-0 No 42827 stands on a centre road at Worcester (Shrub Hill) station in the early 1960's. Popularly referred to as 'Crabs', the class was designed by Hughes and built under the direction of Fowler in 1926. Some were rebuilt with Reidinger rotary valve gear in 1953. Allocated to 21A Saltley for many a year, No 42827 moved to 8H Birkenhead in June 1964, surviving until August 1965. (Tim Farebrother)

4) Quite what 82C Swindon based GWR 5700 Class 0-6-0PT No 9790 is doing at Cardiff (General) on station pilot duties on 7th April 1962 is somewhat of a mystery. The only logical conclusion is that it had been seconded by the powers-that-be at 86C Cardiff (Canton) following an overhaul at Caerphilly Works! No 9790 remained on Swindon's books until November 1964, moving to 83C Westbury. It was condemned from there in September 1965. (R.Picton)

25) Under a super summer sky the peace of Sapperton is shattered by the passing of GWR *Castle* Class 4-6-0 No 5036 *Lyonshall Castle* as it sweeps down the Golden Valley towards Stroud with a Paddington to Gloucester express on 16th June 1962. Based at 81A Old Oak Common, *Lyonshall Castle*, paired with a straight-sided tender, was equipped with a double chimney in December 1960. Withdrawal for No 5036 came three months after this picture was taken. (N.E.Preedy)

6) Sporting a small 'lion-on-wheel' logo on its side-tank, GWR 5400 Class 0-6-0PT No 5407 stands out of steam in the yard of its home shed at 84C Banbury on 19th September 1954. Behind No 5407 is another resident of 84C in the shape of GWR 4300 Class 2-6-0 No 6387. No 5407 spent the remainder of its working life based at Banbury, being withdrawn from there in June 1960. Despatched to Barry Docks in November 1960 it was cut up by Woodhams. (B.K.B.Green)

7) Deserted platforms at St.Austell station greet the arrival of 83F Truro based GWR *Grange* Class 4-6-0 No 6828 *Trellech Grange* which is in charge of a down local passenger train on 16th August 1959. Once of 84F Stourbridge, 87E Landore (Swansea) and 87F Llanelly, *Trellech Grange* had been at 83F since November 1958. In September 1961 it was ousted by the ever growing presence of diesel traction in Cornwall and drafted to 84B Oxley. (Peter Hay)

28) 84A Wolverhampton (Stafford Road) was best known for its top-link passenger locomotives, but also maintained a small stud of GWR 2-6-2 Tanks, one of which was 3150 Class No 3160 (introduced in 1907) pictured in the shed yard at Stafford Road on 12th October 1952 with a resident GWR *Castle* Class 4-6-0 No 5070 *Sir Daniel Gooch* (built in June 1938) as a neighbour. No 3160 was withdrawn well before the fifties drew to an end. (B.K.B.Green)

29) Although of Midland Railway origin and belonging to the London Midland Region (22A), Bristol Barrow Road shed became the property of the Western Region on 23rd February 1958 being coded 82E. A trio of self-conscious looking railwaymen pose to have their photograph taken in front of GWR *Grange* Class 4-6-0 No 6869 *Resolven Grange* (81C Southall) in the yard at Barrow Road in the company of an unidentified LMS *Jubilee* Class 4-6-0 on 21st May 1963. (D.K.Jones)

0) Reflection time at Birmingham (Snow Hill) on 5th September 1962 where for a week GWR *King* Class 4-6-0 No 6002 *King William IV*, from 84A Wolverhampton (Stafford Road), was on show to the public to mark the end of the class on the Paddington expresses. During the previous day *King William IV* was commandeered to take over from a failed diesel and worked an express to Wolverhampton. After withdrawal it was cut up by Cox & Danks, Langley Green. (Author's collection)

1) A busy scene at Oxford station in April 1964. 81E Didcot allocated GWR *Modified Hall* Class 4-6-0 No 7917 *North Aston Hall* is in charge of York to Bournemouth express. Standing on a through road next to *North Aston Hall* is one of the last surviving 4300 Class 2-6-0's No 6367, another Didcot steed, at the head of a partially fitted freight. No 6367, seven months away from condemnation, has a chalked number on its smokebox door. (I.J.Hodson)

32) A feather of steam rises from the safety valves of GWR *Grange* Class 4-6-0 No 6840 *Hazeley Grange*, a visitor to 84G Shrewsbury from 86G Pontypool Road as it stands by the coaling stage - circa 1954. *Hazeley Grange* was to remain faithful to Pontypool Road shed until June 1963 when it was transferred to 87A Neath. A final transfer took place in June 1964 when No 6840 moved the short distance to 87F Llanelly. Withdrawal came in February 1965. (R.S.Carpenter)

33) The cathedral-like interior of Bristol (Temple Meads) station hosts the presence of 55A Leeds (Holbeck) allocated LMS Class 5 4-6-0 No 44757 as it simmers gently with an express next to some over-loaded barrows in the late fifties. No 44757 is fitted with Caprotti valve gear, Timken roller bearings and a double chimney. Leeds (Holbeck) shed retained the services of No 44757 until September 1961 when it was acquired by the LMR at 8M Southport. (R.S.Carpenter)

34) Photographed near to New Passage Halt, closed during 1964, an immaculate looking GWR 4500 Class 2-6-2T No 5546, of 82A Bristol (Temple Meads), heads the 2.30pm Severn Beach to Temple Meads local passenger service consisting of four non-corridor carriages on a sun-filled 12th May 1958. No 5546 departed for pastures new at 83C Exeter (St.Davids) four months later. It also served at 83F Truro and 87H Neyland prior to withdrawal. (N.E.Preedy)

35) Looking in fine external fettle GWR 5700 Class 0-6-0PT No 7708 stands lifeless in a section of the yard at its home shed of 81D Reading on 14th September 1953, a depot it was to remain at until condemnation in June 1960. After a period of storage at Swindon Works No 7708 undertook a final (one-way) journey to South Wales at the infamous scrapyard at Cashmores, Newport, a firm responsible for the scrapping of many fine locomotives. (D.K.Jones)

36) Hemmed between two other locomotives a rather work-stained GWR *Hall* Class 4-6-0 No 6908 *Downham Hall*, from 82A Bristol (Bath Road), stands out of steam in bright sunshine in a section of the large yard at 81A Old Oak Common on 2nd September 1951. Later in its life *Downham Hall* had a lengthy spell at 82B St.Philip's Marsh, from September 1959 to June 1964 when 82B closed. Its last abode was at 82E Bristol Barrow Road, being withdrawn in July 1965. (B.K.B.Green)

37) In green livery BR Class 4 4-6-0 No 75025 (85A Worcester) in charge of a freight train is captured on film at Malvern Wells station in December 1960. Once of 82C Swindon, No 75025 had been allocated to Worcester shed from November 1957 to August 1960 when it moved to 89C Machynlleth. Three months later it was back at Worcester again, this time until January 1964. After two further transfers it ended its days at 85A in December 1965. (Tim Farebrother)

38) On a sunny summer's day in 1957 GWR 2800 Class 2-8-0 No 3862, of 83D Laira (Plymouth), finds a path between express workings and plods its way along on Dainton Bank with a loose-coupled freight train. Rendered redundant at Laira shed in July 1962, No 3862 found a new home at 88A Cardiff (Canton). Two months later it was on the move again, this time to 88L Cardiff East Dock. Withdrawal came in February 1965, from 6C Croes Newydd. (Eric Light)

39) Despite the mass condemnations on the same date there were plenty of steam locomotives under various stages of overhaul inside 'A' Shop at Swindon Works on 9th September 1962. Nearest the camera are the cabsides of GWR *Castle* Class 4-6-0 No 7008 *Swansea Castle* (81A Old Oak Common) and GWR *Manor* Class 4-6-0 No 7827 *Lydham Manor* (89D Oswestry). *Lydham Manor* has been a longstanding preserved item on the Paignton-Kingswear line. (J.Schatz)

40) So successful were C.B.Collett's GWR *Castle* Class 4-6-0's, introduced in 1923, that six of the earlier GWR *Stars* were rebuilt to the new design during the next few years. One such locomotive was No 4000 *North Star*, seen departing from Wolverhampton (Low Level) on a northbound express in 1951. Originally built as a 4-4-2 (No 40) in 1906 it was rebuilt as a *Star* in 1909 and as a *Castle* in 1929. Withdrawal came in May 1957 from 87E Landore. (R.S.Carpenter)

41) We switch from the Midlands to the far-flung reaches of Cornwall where the brilliant sunshine and gleam of brass gives a typical Great Western scene of yesteryear. A nine-coach express hauled by GWR *Grange* Class 4-6-0 No 6829 *Burmington Grange* (83A Newton Abbot) passes a line of coaches in a siding when leaving Penzance with an up express on 25th August 1956. This March 1937 engine survived in revenue earning service until November 1965. (N.L.Browne)

42) Not even a GWR safety valve bonnet and numberplates can disguise the unmistakeable appearance of a Great Central Railway Robinson 'R.O.D.' Class 2-8-0! Bright sunshine highlights the grim external condition of No 3040 seen out of steam at its home shed of 85A Worcester on 14th June 1953, by which time there were only twenty-six survivors of the 100 purchased by the GWR after World War One. No 3040 was withdrawn later in the fifties. (B.K.B.Green)

43) An elderly LMS Class 4F 'Duck Six' 0-6-0, No 44560, nears the end of its lengthy career as it is seen in light steam on a track adjacent to the running shed at 85B Gloucester (Horton Road) on 20th June 1965 a depot it had been allocated to since November 1964. This engine was once based on the former Somerset & Dorset Railway, hence the tablet catcher affixed to the locomotive. It was condemned three months after this picture was taken. (N.E.Preedy)

44) A relic of the past, a telegraph pole with its associated clutter of wires, stands sentinel-like as 82A Bristol (Bath Road) based GWR *Hall* Class 4-6-0 No 5950 *Wardley Hall* drifts towards the camera near to Chalford (closed in 1964) with an express during the summer of 1956. Later transfers took *Wardley Hall* to 82B St.Philip's Marsh and 82D Westbury before becoming an early victim to withdrawal in November 1961 from the latter shed. (N.E.Preedy)

45) A West Midlands holiday extra is almost at the start of its lengthy journey to Minehead seen near to Wednesbury on 8th September 1962. In charge of the train is GWR *Hall* Class 4-6-0 No 4951 *Pendeford Hall*, from 84B Oxley. Unlike many of its sister engines *Pendeford Hall* did not succumb to the mass withdrawals of September 1962, instead, shortly after this photograph was taken, it was transferred to 81F Oxford and later to 82C Swindon. (T.R.Amos)

46) Although fully coaled it is probably the end of the road for two members of the mighty GWR *King* Class 4-6-0's based at 86C Cardiff (Canton) on 23rd April 1962. Parked on a dead road with sacked chimneys are Nos 6003 *King George IV* and 6024 *King Edward I*. Both were officially withdrawn in June 1962. No 6003 was cut up at Swindon Works in August 1962, but No 6024 was saved for posterity from Barry Docks in April 1973 by the Quainton Road movement. (R.Picton)

47) The driver and fireman of begrimed BR Class 3 2-6-2T No 82037, of 82E Bristol Barrow Road, smile at the photographer from the cab of their steed at Bristol (Temple Meads) station on 6th September 1963. No 82037 is heading the 5.20pm local passenger to Wells via Yatton. Once of 88C Barry, No 82037 was one of a numerical trio based at 82E on this date, Nos 82036-38. All were condemned from Barrow Road shed in July and August 1965. (R.Picton)

48) With part of the shed building to be seen in the right of the frame, GWR *Castle* Class 4-6-0 No 5014 *Goodrich Castle*, an 81A Old Oak Common engine, rounds the curve and enters Worcester (Shrub Hill) station with a Hereford to Paddington express in August 1961. Paired with a straight-sided tender, *Goodrich Castle* remained at Old Oak until June 1964, moving to 2A Tyseley. Built at Swindon in June 1932, No 5014 was withdrawn in February 1965. (N.E.Preedy)

49) A rather less than clean GWR 4300 Class 2-6-0 No 7340 comes off its home shed at 81E Didcot light engine to take up an unknown duty on a sunny November day in 1963. By this date in time the writing was on the wall for this particular class of engines, being rendered extinct by November 1964. This locomotive was originally numbered No 9318, changing to No 7340 in January 1958. It was condemned in June 1964 and cut up at Birds, Risca. (I.J.Hodson)

50) Originally owned by the Somerset & Dorset Railway the small two-road shed at Templecombe had four shedcodes from 1948 until closure on 7th March 1966, these being 22D, 71H, 82G and 83G. It came under the control of the Western Region from 23rd February 1958 onwards. Noted out of steam in the shed yard on 11th September 1960 is one of its resident LMS Class 3 2-6-2 Tanks, No 41248 which departed from 82G two months later. (A.N.H.Glover)

51) Paired with a straight-sided tender GWR *Castle* Class 4-6-0 No 5011 *Tintagel Castle*, from 81A Old Oak Common, steams out of the London terminus of Paddington with the 9.15am express to Worcester on 6th August 1962. Once of 83A Newton Abbot, *Tintagel Castle* had arrived at 81A via 81D Reading in October 1960. Despite its excellent external condition it was withdrawn from Old Oak the following month after completing 1,732,565 miles. (R.Picton)

52) Its pipework 'Westernised', LMS Class 8F 2-8-0 No 48475 is photographed in a remote section of the yard of its home shed at 84F Stourbridge on 6th May 1962. A once longstanding resident of 82B St.Philip's Marsh, No 48475 moved to the Midlands at 84E Tyseley in June 1959. It returned to 82B in August of the following year before moving to Stourbridge in March 1962. It was withdrawn from revenue earning service from 2B Oxley in October 1966. (N.E.Preedy)

3) A bedraggled resident of 81D Reading, GWR 9400 Class 0-6-0PT No 8464, is about to take refreshment in the shed yard at 81D on a dull 29th September 1963 three months before being rendered redundant and withdrawn from service with scrapping taking place at Swindon Works in February 1964. In the left hand background we can make out the cab of another 81D engine, GWR *Hall* Class 4-6-0 No 5932 *Haydon Hall* which moved to 81F Oxford later in 1963. (R.S.Carpenter)

4) As a railwayman chats to the footplate crew a male traveller looks unmoved as he is captured on film at Shrewsbury station on 16th September 1962. The main subject of the photographer is locally based GWR 4300 Class 2-6-0 No 7314 which has steam to spare after arriving with a passenger service. For many years an 87F Llanelly locomotive, No 7314 was drafted to 84J Croes Newydd in June 1960 where it remained until September 1961, moving to 89A. (D.K.Jones)

55) Throughout British Railways the classic 'engine and brake' was an everyday occurrence as they scurried off to a multitude of unknown destinations to set about their work for the rostered shift. One such pairing is noted at Birmingham (Snow Hill) in 1957 as 84B Oxley based GWR 5600 Class 0-6-2T No 5684 heads in the direction of Hockley and Wolverhampton. From January 1958 until September 1963, No 5684 worked from sheds in South Wales. (R.S.Carpenter)

56) Remaining in the Midlands we move south to the once busy but long demolished depot at Banbury, coded 84C from 1949 until 9th September 1963 when it was recoded 2D by the London Midland Region authorities. With a large gasometer in the background, another 84B Oxley locomotive is captured on film in August 1958. Looking fresh from overhaul is GWR *Hall* Class 4-6-0 No 5916 *Trinity Hall* which is awaiting its next duty in the shed yard. (L.C.Jacks)

7) Sunlight and shadow as the weeds take over outside 82B St.Philip's Marsh shed in Bristol on 4th October 1955 where 'R.O.D' Class 2-8-0 No 3017 is noted out of steam. Note the boiler mountings and top feed fitted at Swindon Works after the locomotive was purchased from the government, newly constructed in 1919. St.Philip's Marsh, opened by the GWR in July 1910, was a standard, two turntable unit shed with the usual facilities. (D.K.Jones)

8) Looking the worse for wear 88A Cardiff (Canton) GWR *Hall* Class 4-6-0 No 4953 *Pitchford Hall* passes through Sydney Gardens, Bath with an express on 8th September 1962, the day before Canton closed to steam and No 4953 was transferred to 88L Cardiff East Dock. Despite its condition it is surprising that it survived until April 1963. After withdrawal it languished in store at East Dock and Barry Docks until saved for posterity in more recent times (D.K.Jones)

59) Piles of discarded ash litter the foreground outside the shed at 85A Worcester where one of its residents, BR Class 3 2-6-2T No 82030 is in steam in October 1957 in the company of a visitor from 81A Old Oak Common in the shape of GWR *Castle* Class 4-6-0 No 7016 *Chester Castle*. No 82030 tended to move around a lot in its short career serving from a number of sheds including 85B Gloucester (Horton Road) and 83G Templecombe. (N.E.Preedy)

60) Nigh on maximum track occupation alongside the running shed at 82E Bristol Barrow Road where a dozen or so steam engines, mostly of the GWR variety, are in steam as they await their next rostered duties on a murky 1st November 1964. The only locomotive which can be positively identified is LMS Class 4F 0-6-0 No 44102, once of 82F Bath Green Park, having been condemned two months earlier. Today, there is little or no trace of Barrow Road shed. (R.Picton)

1) The long preserved GWR 1400 Class 0-4-2T No 1450 waits impatiently at Exeter St.Davids station with a local passenger train in the summer of 1962. Once of 81B Slough, No 1450 was transferred to 81F Oxford in August 1959 a depot it was to stay at before moving to 83C St.Davids shed in July 1962. Later moves took it to 83B Taunton, 83E Yeovil and 83D Exmouth Junction. After withdrawal in May 1965 it was earmarked for the Dart Valley Railway. (R.W.Hinton)

2) With the Malvern Hills providing a splendid backdrop a somewhat less than clean GWR *Modified Hall* Class 4-6-0 No 6984 *Owsden Hall*, from 85A Worcester, provides the motive power for the daily pick-up at Malvern Wells station in the summer of 1960. Withdrawn from service in December 1965 from 81F Oxford, No 6984 was fated to be rescued from Barry Docks in October 1986 after rusting for over twenty years. It now lives on in private hands. (Tim Farebrother)

63) High pressure steam issues from the safety valves of BR Class 4 2-6-0 No 76025, from 70F Bournemouth and minus shedplate, as it stands in bright sunshine outside the fragile looking wooden built running shed at 82F Bath Green Park in 1964. Prior to being allocated to Green Park shed in May 1961, No 76025 was based for many years at 71A Eastleigh. After withdrawal in October 1965, No 76025 was stored for a while prior to being despatched for scrapping. (M.Wood)

64) 21A Saltley based LMS Class 5 4-6-0 No 44962 provides more than adequate power for the three-coach 5.05pm local passenger train from Bristol (Temple Meads) to Birmingham (New Street) seen near to Clay Bottom on 4th July 1964. After being a longstanding resident at 21A for many a year, No 44962 had a number of moves from May 1963 onwards serving from 15C Leicester (Midland), 16C Derby, 16F Burton, 8F Springs Branch Wigan and 9D Newton Heath. (R.Picton)

65) With a mixed bag of empty coaching stock in the background, GWR *Castle* Class 4-6-0 No 5033 *Broughton Castle* is a visitor to 84E Tyseley from 81F Oxford on 23rd June 1961. Constructed at Swindon Works in May 1935 *Broughton Castle* was modified with a double chimney in October 1960 and prior to June 1958 it was allocated to 84K Chester GWR. No 5033 was to fall victim to the mass withdrawals of September 1962 and was cut up two months later. (L.C.Jacks)

66) The notorious 'dump' at Swindon Works was a sad place for steam enthusiasts as locomotives waited their turn for the cutter's torch. Some engines were stored for months and even years before being reduced to scrap. Such is the case with GWR 3100 Class 2-6-2T No 3100 which was stored at Swindon from May 1957 until February 1961 after withdrawal from 86F Tondu. No 3100 is noted rusting away on the 'dump' on 16th October 1960. (N.L.Browne)

67) Matched with a straight-sided tender, GWR *Hall* Class 4-6-0 No 4985 *Allesley Hall*, of 83B Taunton, is seen far from home at rest in the shed yard at 84G Shrewsbury after working an excursion in 1958. For many years *Allesley Hall* was part of the scenery at 83B until February 1963 when it was drafted to 86G Pontypool Road. Later transfers took it to 85B Gloucester (Horton Road) and 87A Neath prior to withdrawal in September 1964. (D.K.Jones)

68) GWR *Castle* Class 4-6-0 No 5068 *Beverston Castle*, based at 82C Swindon, heads a milk/parcels train at Wapley on the Bath to Bristol main line on 16th May 1958. Built in June 1938 *Beverston Castle* was later modified with a double chimney in February 1961. Transferred from Swindon to 81F Oxford in May 1962, No 5068 was yet another victim of the mass condemnations in September 1962 after completing 1,081,514 miles. It was cut up at the end of 1962. (D.K.Jones)

69) A quartet of repeater signals look down upon Gloucester (Central) station which is bathed in sunlight and shadow on 22nd June 1952. Bearing the logo of its former owner is GWR 1400 Class 0-4-2T No 1413, a locally based locomotive, which is powering a Gloucester to Cheltenham auto-train. These useful engines were to be seen on many parts of the Western Region system and some examples were to be found at 6C Birkenhead and 34E Neasdon. (R.W.Hinton)

70) Complete with a straight-sided tender, GWR *Castle* Class 4-6-0 No 5038 *Morlais Castle* looks in pristine condition as a member of the footplate crew takes things easy at Birmingham (Snow Hill) station on 12th July 1962. *Morlais Castle*, from 81F Oxford, is in charge of a Bournemouth to Wolverhampton (Low Level) express. Transferred to 81D Reading in October of the same year, No 5038 was taken out of service in September 1963. (J.Schatz)

71) Locally based GWR *Manor* Class 4-6-0 No 7806 *Cockington Manor* is photographed at rest outside the six-road shed at 83A Newton Abbot on 6th September 1959 shortly before being transferred to 83E St.Blazey. Apart from the locoshed there was also a large workshop and carriage and wagon works at Newton Abbot. With the mass introduction of diesels in the south-west in the late fifties/early sixties 83A lost most of its allocated steam by mid-1962. (B.K.B.Green)

72) Equipped with a double chimney in February 1958, GWR *Castle* Class 4-6-0 No 7004 *Eastnor Castle*, from 81D Reading, is only three short months away from withdrawal when seen in steam in the shed yard at 81E Didcot on 25th October 1963. Constructed in June 1946 *Eastnor Castle* had a working life of less then eighteen years when withdrawn after covering only 876,349 miles. It was scrapped at its birthplace at Swindon in February 1964. (D.K.Jones)

73) The workhorses of the Great Western and Western Region of British Railways were the once numerous GWR 5700 Class 0-6-0 Pannier Tanks. Employed on station pilot duties, No 3747, shedded locally at 86A Newport (Ebbw Junction), departs from Newport (High Street) with a mixed bag of stock in 1961. Once of 86H Aberbeeg, No 3747 had been at 86A since October 1959. It was taken out of traffic from Ebbw Junction shed in February 1965. (R.W.Hinton)

74) A timeless scene of the rural railways that were once common throughout the land. The pioneer GWR 1400 Class 0-4-2T No 1400 passes what appears to be a semi-derelict shanty-town dwelling at Stanton Crossing on the Highbridge branch with a local passenger working on 9th May 1949. All in all a total of seventy-five 1400 series units were constructed and all but seven were still in active service by the beginning of 1957. (S.L.C.Philips)

75) We switch from the Somerset countryside to the Welsh Valleys and find ourselves 'on shed' at 87D Swansea East Dock on 23rd April 1961 where a number of tank engine types are parked in the depot yard. Nearest the camera is GWR 5600 Class 0-6-2T No 5675 a resident of 87D and destined for withdrawal from 87F Llanelly in December 1964. We can also identify GWR 5700 Class 0-6-0PT No 6764 which was condemned from East Dock shed in December 1963. (A.N.H.Glover)

6) A rare photograph of the famous but ill-fated GWR *Castle* Class 4-6-0 No 111 *Viscount Churchill* which was rebuilt in September 1924 from the 1908 built Pacific *The Great Bear*. *Viscount Churchill* became the eleventh *Castle* to be built and is seen fully coaled and in steam outside the shed at 81D Reading in 1952. Equipped with a tall chimney and small front cab windows No 111 was withdrawn in July 1953 after completing 1,989,628 miles. (D.K.Jones)

7) With the Cowley Bridge Inn in the right of the frame looking like a 'marzipan house', GWR 4500 Class 2-6-2T No 4589 rattles over the junction for Barnstaple and Ilfracombe at Cowley Bridge on the outskirts of Exeter with a down passenger train on 1st August 1959. No 4589, from 83C Exeter (St.Davids), had for a time worked from sheds in South Wales. Transferred to 83D Laira (Plymouth) in June 1960 it was withdrawn three months later. (D.K.Jones)

78) A famous location on a wet and miserable looking 'summer's' day on 20th June 1954 where a few holidaymakers brave the conditions as they take a stroll along the promenade at Dawlish. Coasting into the station is an up express in the capable hands of GWR *Hall* Class 4-6-0 No 5936 *Oakley Hall*, from 81A Old Oak Common. *Oakley Hall* later served from the sheds at 81D Reading and 85B Gloucester (Horton Road) before withdrawal in January 1965. (D.K.Jones)

79) On a summer Saturday in 1960 LMS Class 4F 0-6-0 No 44528 (17B Burton) trundles through Defford station, situated between Bromsgrove and Ashchurch and closed in 1965, with a southbound freight. This class of engines was introduced in 1924 and had a very 'Midland' appearance with a distinctive 'clank' made by the motion which contributed towards their nickname of 'Duck Six'. Drafted to 16G Westhouses in October 1964, No 44528 was withdrawn in May 1965. (Tim Farebrother)

30) The platforms at Chalford are all but deserted with the exception of a solitary railwayman as GWR 1400 Class 0-4-2T No 1453, sporting a home-made front numberplate, blows off steam at the head of the 2.05pm local passenger train from Gloucester on 26th May 1963 the year before closure under the Beeching axe. Based at 85B Gloucester (Horton Road) since a move from 84C Banbury in August 1962, No 1453 survived there until November 1964. (J.Schatz)

31) On the subject of Gloucester this next photograph is taken outside the shed at Horton Road (85B) on 16th October 1965 where the sole surviving GWR *Castle* Class 4-6-0 No 7029 *Clun Castle* has been spruced-up in readiness to work the return train of the 'GWR Cavalcade' the following day. Like No 1453 in the previous picture, *Clun Castle* also has a home-made front numberplate. Following withdrawal in December 1965, No 7029 was actively preserved. (W.Potter)

82) GWR 5700 Class 0-6-0PT No 9789, from 81C Southall, approaches a boarded crossing at Colnbrook on the West Drayton to Staines branch on 25th August 1956. This station was doomed to die in 1965. No 9789 remained on the books at Southall until January 1962 when it was drafted to 81D Reading. It also served from 81A Old Oak Common and 81F Oxford before its demise in December 1965. In April 1966 it was despatched to Wards, Briton Ferry for scrapping. (N.E.Preedy)

3) Two railwaymen look unenthusiastically towards the camera near to the crumbling edge of a platform at Swindon station on 25th April 1954. Inside the smoke-blackened station are a duet of GWR Class 2P 'Dukedog' 4-4-0's Nos 9023 and 9011 which are harnessed in tandem at the head of an RCTS special consisting of Southern Railway stock. Note the ATC ramp on the up through road. Nos 9011/23, both from 82C Swindon, were withdrawn in July 1957. (Peter Hay)

4) A trio of GWR 2-6-2 Tank engines are lined up in the yard at 84E Tyseley on 15th July 1951. In the centre of the trio is 3150 Class No 3151 for which time is running out. The rugged locomotives from this class were somewhat advanced for their day and many spent their working lives on banking duties. However, No 3151 was mainly employed on local passenger work in the Birmingham area until withdrawn from service in February 1952. (B.K.B.Green)

85) It is the end of the line for GWR 4500 Class 2-6-2T No 5520 seen stripped of its numberplates and dumped amidst the weeds in a siding at Whitland in June 1963 some nine months after condemnation from 87H Neyland. The following month it was despatched to Hayes, Bridgend for scrapping. Whitland depot (closed in December 1963), a sub-shed of Neyland, adopted the code of 87H when the latter closed three months earlier. (N.L.Browne)

86) Smoke, grime and discarded ashes are all part of the everyday scene at 84A Wolverhampton (Stafford Road) in the late fifties. Several locomotives are in view outside the two straight running sheds and in the foreground is GWR *Castle* Class 4-6-0 No 5043 *Earl of Mount Edgcumbe*, from 81A Old Oak Common and equipped with a double chimney. Withdrawn in December 1963, No 5043 was rescued from Barry Docks In August 1973 by the Birmingham Railway Museum. (G.M.Gardiner)

7) Three 'ex.works' oil headlamps are tucked away neatly on the running plate of GWR 5700 Class 0-6-0PT No 7748 which is being employed on station pilot duties at Westbury, Wilts on a sunny 13th August 1959. No 7748 is based at the near-at-hand shed, coded 82D, situated to the south side of the main line to the west of the station, a five minute walk for spotters on foot. No 7748 was withdrawn from 82D in April 1961 and cut up at Swindon. (N.E.Preedy)

8) Sporting the train reporting number and the headcode of *The Cornishman*, GWR *Castle* Class 4-6-0 No 5085 *Evesham Abbey*, from 82A Bristol (Bath Road), pounds along on Dainton bank on a dull summer's day in 1958. *Evesham Abbey* moved the short distance to 82B St.Philip's Marsh after the closure of 82A to steam in September 1960. It later served from the sheds at 81D Reading, 87A Neath and 87F Llanelly before returning to 82B in March 1963. (D.K.Jones)

89) GWR *Hall* Class 4-6-0 No 5950 *Wardley Hall*, of 83D Laira (Plymouth), is way off the beaten track as it heads northwards through Solihull station on the outskirts of Birmingham with a train of perishables from Plymouth in the late fifties. How this scene has changed over the years. The four tracks are now down to two. Gone are the goods yard and signalbox and all of the buildings on the right hand platform have long been demolished. (R.S.Carpenter)

90) A dull day in Bristol in 1959. 82B St.Philip's Marsh allocated GWR *Grange* Class 4-6-0 No 6827 *Llanfrechfa Grange* is at rest longside the running shed at 82A Bath Road on a track leading to the turntable. After closure to steam in September 1962, Bath Road was converted into a diesel depot, but was all but completely closed during 1995. *Llanfrechfa Grange* survived in service until September 1965, being withdrawn from 84B Oxley. (D.K.Jones)

1) With a fine array of lower quadrant signals and a locomotive in the background a bedraggled looking 83B Taunton based GWR *Hall* Class 4-6-0 No 4903 *Astley Hall*, minus shedplate, passes the large water tank as it makes its way onto 83C Exeter St.Davids shed on a dull and wet summer's day in 1963. No 4903 was allocated to a variety of sheds from January 1957 up until being taken out of service from 85A Worcester in October 1964. (G.H.Truran)

2) A splendid panoramic view of the northern approaches to Oxford station with its gantry of signals and signalbox. Heavy freight locomotive, GWR 2800 Class 2-8-0 No 3850, from 2D Banbury, heads southwards with a mixed freight in August 1964. Prior to withdrawal in August 1965, No 3850 also served from the sheds at 6E Oswestry and 6C Croes Newydd. An inmate of the infamous Barry Docks, No 3850 has since been salvaged for posterity. (I.J.Hodson)

93) Resident to 83G Penzance, GWR *Hall* Class 4-6-0 No 5985 *Mostyn Hall* is smartly turned out as it departs from the Penzance area with a short up parcels/gas train on 21st August 1956. This October 1938 built engine made its leave of 83G in April 1958 moving to a new abode at 84B Oxley. Later in life it also served from 81C Southall, 81A Old Oak Common and 81F Oxford. Withdrawn in September 1963 it was later scrapped at Cashmores, Newport. (N.L.Browne)

94) Looking in pristine condition GWR *Castle* Class 4-6-0 No 5021 *Whittington Castle*, newly transferred to 83D Laira (Plymouth) from 83C Exeter St.Davids, is ready to take up its next express working from Paddington in the yard at 81A Old Oak Common on a damp 10th April 1957. Constructed at Swindon Works in August 1932, No 5021 was also based at 86C Cardiff - Canton (twice) and 82B St.Philip's Marsh before condemnation in September 1962. (N.L.Browne)

95) Safety valves lifting gently, 84E Tyseley based GWR *Hall* Class 4-6-0 No 5927 *Guild Hall* stands near to the coaling stage at the four-road September 1906 built shed at Leamington, coded 84D and 2L, on a sunny day in 1951. The depot closed completely on 14th June 1965 with the majority of its surviving locomotives being transferred to Tyseley. *Guild Hall*, for many years a Tyseley steed, succumbed to withdrawal in October 1964. (B.K.B.Green)

96) Smoke and steam are swept sidewards by a strong wind as GWR *County* Class 4-6-0 No 1007 *County of Brecknock*, from 83F Truro, gets to grips with an up express as it departs from Gwinear Road station in August 1957. Note the GWR 4500 Class 2-6-2T in the Helston branch platform in the left of the picture. *County of Brecknock*, modified with a double chimney earlier in the year, was transferred to 83C Exeter St.Davids in September 1959. (Peter Hay)

97) The Midland Railway influence is more than obvious as former Somerset & Dorset Joint Railway Class 7F 2-8-0 No 53808, of 82F Bath Green Park and in ex.works condition, is photographed at Evercreech Junction on 30th September 1962. The first six members of the class were constructed at Derby Works in 1914 followed by five others from Robert Stephenson & Co., in 1925. No 53808 was rescued from Barry Docks in October 1970 by the West Somerset Railway. (D.K.Jones)

98) Escaping steam from the safety valves of GWR 1400 Class 0-4-2T No 1444 disturbs the rustic tranquility of Chalford station, terminus of the Stroud Valley auto-service from Gloucester, on an idyllic day in May 1964. No 1444, looking in fine external fettle, had been based at 85B Gloucester (Horton Road) since transferring from 81F Oxford in December 1963. It was condemned from 85B in October 1964, being cut up at Hayes, Bridgend in April 1965. (N.E.Preedy)

99) Quite a large selection of GWR *County* Class 4-6-0's were allocated to Shrewsbury shed over the years and two of them are noted in the yard at 84G on 3rd April 1960, these being Nos 1017 *County of Hereford* and 1026 *County of Salop*, of which the latter is receiving some attention. Both were equipped with double chimneys, in March 1959 and October 1958 respectively. No 1026 was withdrawn in September 1962 followed by No 1017 later in the year. (D.K.Jones)

100) GWR 4200 Class 2-8-0T No 5240, allocation not known, is photographed at rest in the shed yard at 81D Reading - circa 1952. Records show is that in January 1957 No 5240 was allocated to 87D Swansea East Dock. In August 1959 it was drafted to 87F Llanelly, followed by a move to its final home at 86J/88J Aberdare in September 1960. Withdrawal for No 5240 came in February 1964 and it was scrapped two months later at Hayes, Bridgend. (D.K.Jones)

101) On a sun-filled 19th July 1954, GWR *Castle* Class 4-6-0 No 5082 *Swordfish*, an 81A Old Oak Common steed, passes the level crossing and enters Exeter St.Davids station with the down *Torbay Express* from Paddington. Constructed at Swindon as *Powis Castle* three months before the outbreak of World War Two, No 5082 was renamed *Swordfish* in January 1941. Withdrawn from Old Oak in July 1962 it was cut up at Cashmores, Great Bridge at the end of 1962. (A.Wakefield)

102) Hummocks of discarded ash litter the foreground as a longstanding and well turned out resident of 81D Reading, GWR *Modified Hall* Class 4-6-0 No 7914 *Lleweni Hall* rests in the yard of its home shed on 14th June 1959. *Lleweni Hall* was destined to remain at 81D until April 1964, thereafter moving on to three different homes at 82B St.Philip's Marsh, 82E Bristol Barrow Road and 81F Oxford. It was withdrawn from the latter in December 1965. (N.E.Preedy)

103) Sunlight and shadow at Plymouth (North Road) where 83D Laira (Plymouth) based GWR *Castle* Class 4-6-0 No 7022 *Hereford Castle* has been reduced to taking charge of a local passenger train on 24th June 1958. Equipped with a double chimney in December of the previous year *Hereford Castle* had been transferred to Laira from 86C Cardiff (Canton) in January 1957. It was fated to be one of the last *Castles* in service, being condemned in June 1965. (N.E.Preedy)

104) Many miles adrift of its normal haunts, 89D Oswestry allocated GWR 2251 Class 0-6-0 No 3208 drifts along in a flurry of steam with a rake of wagons at Priestfield in the West Midlands on 7th September 1962. Transferred to 89C Machynlleth in June 1963, No 3208 worked out its last days from there, being withdrawn in May 1965. It was stored at 89C for two months before being despatched for scrapping at the Central Wagon Co., Wigan. (T.R.Amos)

105) It is approaching fifteen minutes past ten in the morning and the opposite platform is packed with expectant passengers as they await the arrival of their train at Taunton. The focus of attention of the photographer is of locally based (83B) GWR 4300 Class 2-6-0 No 7326 which is in charge of a local passenger turn on 24th June 1962. Once of 85C Hereford (twice), 83C Exeter St.Davids and 83D Laira (Plymouth), No 7326 had been at 83B since March 1961. (D.K.Jones)

106) Coal is stockpiled at the rarely photographed shed at Kidderminster on 14th June 1953, coded 85D, 84G and 2P in BR days. In the left of the frame is BR Class 3 2-6-2T No 82008. In the right of the picture, from left to right are, former Cleobury Mortimer and Ditton Priors Light Railway 0-6-0PT No 29, GWR 2021 Class 0-6-0PT No 2144 and GWR 5101 Class 2-6-2T No 4153. Kidderminster shed, a two-road affair, closed on 10th August 1964. (N.E.Preedy)

107) Looking in splendid external condition GWR *Castle* Class 4-6-0 No 5024 *Carew Castle* is fully coaled and ready for its next rostered duty in the yard of its home shed at 83A Newton Abbot on a sunny 15th April 1956. *Carew Castle* was noted by the author on shed at 83A on 29th April 1962 shortly before withdrawal along with sister engines Nos 4098 *Kidwelly Castle*, 5003 *Lulworth Castle*, 5055 *Earl of Eldon*, 5098 *Clifford Castle* and 7029 *Clun Castle*. (D.K.Jones)

108) Rows of domestic dwellings look down upon the railway scene at 88C Barry on 31st August 1952 where the yard is packed with tank engine power. Three of the locomotives on view can be identified as GWR 5700 Class 0-6-0PT No 6712, GWR 1901 Class 0-6-0PT No 2008 and GWR 5700 Class 0-6-0PT No 6758. Of the three, No 2008 was the first to be withdrawn in March 1958, from 6C Birkenhead, followed by No 6712 in July 1960 and No 6758 in June 1962. (B.K.B.Green)

109) GWR *Hall* Class 4-6-0 No 5923 *Colston Hall*, from 81A Old Oak Common, powers a troop train special (Z71) through Malvern Wells in 1960. There being a number of army camps in Wales it was not surprising to see the odd troop train heading in that direction in those days. *Colston Hall* is seen passing the site of the original station which burnt down in the 1860's and was rebuilt nearer to the Malvern Hills. No 5923 was withdrawn in December 1963. (Tim Farebrother)

10) Work-stained GWR 2800 Class 2-8-0 No 3836, of 89A Shrewsbury, passes over the river Severn at Over Junction with a
   Class 8 loose-coupled freight train on a dull day in 1963. Once of 81C Southall and 86C Cardiff (Canton), No 3836 had been
   at Shrewsbury shed since September 1959. It was drafted to 87A Neath in November 1963. Its final abode was at 82E Bristol
   Barrow Road (December 1964) being condemned from there in November 1965. (P.A.Bridgman)

11) GWR *Castle* Class 4-6-0 No 4073 *Caerphilly Castle* stands beneath the lengthy footbridge at 86C Cardiff (Canton) on
   14th September 1958 which had been the home for this engine since a move from 82A Bristol (Bath Road) in February 1957.
   Built in August 1923 *Caerphilly Castle* was withdrawn from Canton in May 1960 after completing 1,910,730 miles.
   Preserved in the Science Museum at Kensington since June 1961 it recently moved to Didcot. (N.E.Preedy)

112) At the conclusion of its journey from Plymouth, GWR *Hall* Class 4-6-0 No 4992 *Crosby Hall*, from 83D Laira, steams into Penzance station with a lengthy local passenger train on 21st August 1956. Between this date and being taken out of service in April 1965, *Crosby Hall* worked from a number of different sheds, including 83A Newton Abbot, 83C Exeter St.Davids, 83B Taunton, 85B Gloucester (Horton Road) and 86E Severn Tunnel Junction. (N.L.Browne)

113) Three members of the shed staff at 85B Gloucester (Horton Road) pose for the camera in between shunting duties in the yard along with one of the inmates of 85B, GWR 9400 Class 0-6-0PT No 9441 on 3rd June 1951. No 9441 was still to be found at Horton Road many years later, finally taking its leave of the depot in January 1961, moving to a new abode at 87D Swansea East Dock. Withdrawn in November 1963 it was scrapped at Wards, Briton Ferry. (N.E.Preedy)

14) Copper, brass and paintwork gleam and glisten from two locomotives which are fresh from overhaul from the 'factory' at Swindon on 2nd December 1951. Waiting to be reunited with their tenders are GWR *Castle* Class 4-6-0 No 7004 *Eastnor Castle* (81A Old Oak Common) and GWR *King* Class 4-6-0 No 6010 *King Charles I*, from 83D Laira (Plymouth). Both engines were later modified with double chimneys, No 7004 (February 1958) and 6010 (March 1956). (R.W.Hinton)

15) Sunlight and shadow at Bristol (Temple Meads) station on 30th August 1959, where locally based (82A Bath Road) GWR *County* Class 4-6-0 No 1011 *County of Chester* lifts its safety valves whilst at the head of a local passenger working. Transferred 'up the road' to 82B St.Philip's Marsh in September 1960, *County of Chester* was on the move again in November 1963, this time to 82C Swindon. It was the last working example being withdrawn in November 1964. (R.W.Hinton)

116) A mixture of wheel arrangements in the depot yard at 89D Oswestry on 2nd September 1962. Nearest the camera is a local inmate in the shape of GWR 2251 Class 0-6-0 No 3208 behind which is an unidentified member of the LMS Ivatt Class 2 2-6-0's. Adjacent to No 3208 is GWR 7400 Class 0-6-0PT No 7440 which is a visitor to Oswestry from 89B Croes Newydd. Although looking in fine fettle this latter engine was withdrawn the following month. (J.Schatz)

117) Looking every inch a pedigree, GWR *Castle* Class 4-6-0 No 7001 *Sir James Milne*, a local steed, is noted in the yard at its home shed at 81A Old Oak Common on 3rd January 1954. Peeping out behind the front end of No 7001 is GWR *Grange* Class 4-6-0 No 6866 *Morfa Grange*, from 84E Tyseley. *Sir James Milne*, built in May 1946, later received a double chimney in September 1960. Drafted to 84B Oxley in September 1963 it was condemned during the same month. (D.K.Jones)

18) With the fireman atop the tender in the left background sorting out his coal supplies, two youthful spotters, complete with baggy trousers, look towards the photographer at Gloucester (Central) station on 9th June 1951. Nearest the camera is GWR 4300 Class 2-6-0 No 6352, of 85C Hereford, which is presumably at the head of a Hereford line local passenger. No 6352 was taken out of service from 86C Cardiff (Canton) in November 1960. (N.E.Preedy)

19) With a cheerful fireman waving an arm from the footplate of his charge, LMS Ivatt Class 4 2-6-0 No 43122 (21A Saltley) heads southward towards Defford with a local service from Birmingham (New Street) to Cheltenham and Gloucester in the early sixties. Once of 53A Hull (Dairycoates), No 43122 had made the move to Saltley depot in May 1959. It was transferred to 1E Bletchley in November 1964 and spent its last days based at 12D Workington. (Tim Farebrother)

120) With a large forest providing a backcloth, GWR 5700 Class 0-6-0PT No 7723, allocated to 85B Gloucester (Horton Road), shunts mineral wagons near to the isolated outpost of Staple Edge Halt on the Cinderford branch on 25th May 1957. If there was a night shift on the branch it would have been a spooky place for the signalman on his lonely vigil at Staple Edge Halt (closed in 1958). No 7723 managed to soldier on in service until August 1960. (F.Hornby)

21) Sporting the train reporting number (216), GWR *King* Class 4-6-0 No 6012 *King Edward VI* (81A Old Oak Common) pauses at Reading (General) station with a Paddington to Cardiff (General) express on 4th August 1959. Commencing life in April 1928, *King Edward VI* finished its days on the Paddington-Birmingham (Snow Hill)-Wolverhampton (Low Level) services after being transferred to 84A Wolverhampton (Stafford Road) from 81A in April 1962. (Tim Farebrother)

22) On the subject of Stafford Road shed we find ourselves in the yard of the same on 29th October 1963. Although officially closed on the 9th September 1963, Stafford Road hosts 81D Reading based GWR *Castle* Class 4-6-0 No 5018 *St.Mawes Castle*, possibly the last 'live' occupant to use this once busy depot. Today, there is little or nothing to show its previous existence. Note the viaduct in the background which carries the former LNWR main line (P.A.Rowlings)

123) Built in June 1929, GWR *Hall* Class 4-6-0 No 4934 *Hindlip Hall*, from 86C Cardiff (Canton), powers what may possibly be the stock of an express to Cardiff at Paddington station on 30th June 1956. Transferred to 81C Southall in February 1958, *Hindlip Hall* later had spells of residential duty from the sheds at 83A Newton Abbot (twice), 82C Swindon and 83B Taunton. Withdrawn from 83B in September 1962 it languished in store there until May 1964. (F.Hornby)

124) We switch from one side of England to the other and alight at Plymouth (North Road) station where on a dull looking 8th May 1963 we espy GWR *Hall* Class 4-6-0 No 6921 *Borwick Hall*, shedded locally at 83D Laira, at the head of the 6.25am express from Bristol (Temple Meads). To the right of *Borwick Hall*, which survived in service until October 1965 from 81F Oxford, is SR N Class 2-6-0 No 31839 (72A Exmouth Junction) on a portion of the 'A.C.E.'. (J.Schatz)

25) We complete this trio of photographs of the GWR *Hall* Class 4-6-0's with a shot of begrimed No 5962 *Wantage Hall*, of 86G Pontypool Road, which is in steam in the company of an equally begrimed unidentified BR Class 9F 2-10-0 in the shed yard at 82E Bristol Barrow Road on 11th April 1964. The gaunt dwellings in the background look like survivors from the siege of Stalingrad in 1942 rather than homes in Britain in the 'modern' sixties. (D.K.Jones)

26) Deep shadows in the sidings near to one of the running sheds at 89A Shrewsbury on 13th May 1961. Nearest the camera is one of Shrewsbury's inmates, GWR *Castle* Class 4-6-0 No 5070 *Sir Daniel Gooch*, a transfer to the shed from 84A Wolverhampton (Stafford Road) in February 1960. In the right of the picture is GWR *Manor* Class 4-6-0 No 7822 *Foxcote Manor*, an 89D Oswestry engine. No 5070 died in March 1964, whereas No 7822 lives on today in preservation. (D.K.Jones)

127) A line-up of filthy locomotives are stabled near to the coal stage at Wolverhampton's Oxley shed (84B) on a grey 2nd September 1962. Leading the line is GWR 2800 Class 2-8-0 No 3821 (84C Banbury) behind which is an unidentified sister locomotive. In the left of the frame is GWR *Hall* Class 4-6-0 No 5926 *Grotrian Hall*, another Banbury engine, which was withdrawn later in the month. No 3821 survived in revenue earning service until October 1964. (F.Hornby)

128) Shedded at the near-at-hand depot (83C), GWR *Castle* Class 4-6-0 No 4081 *Warwick Castle* simmers at the head of *The Cornishman* express at Exeter St.Davids station on a July day in 1958. No 4081 was only allocated to 83C from June to December 1958, moving on to 82A Bristol (Bath Road). During the latter years of its life it was based in South and West Wales at 87F Lanelly and 87G Carmarthen. It was withdrawn in January 1963. (Eric Light)

29) Hot summer sunshine beats off the platform at Kingswear station on 26th July 1961 as GWR *County* Class 4-6-0 No 1008 *County of Cardigan*, from 83G Penzance, awaits departure with an up express. In September 1962 *County of Cardigan* was drafted away from Penzance to 87H Neyland. Later moves took it to 89A Shrewsbury (March 1963) and 82C Swindon (September 1963). After withdrawal (October 1963) it was scrapped in 1964 at Cashmores, Newport. (D.K.Jones)

30) GWR Dean Goods 0-6-0 No 2350 is noted in light steam in the yard in front of the depot at Lydney on 16th June 1951. This quite large structure was a sub-shed to 85B Gloucester (Horton Road) up until complete closure in October 1963. At one time it was the main depot of the Severn & Wye Railway with a main works and repair shops. Some of the buildings at the shed dated back to the time when there were horse-drawn tramway vehicles in use. (N.E.Preedy)

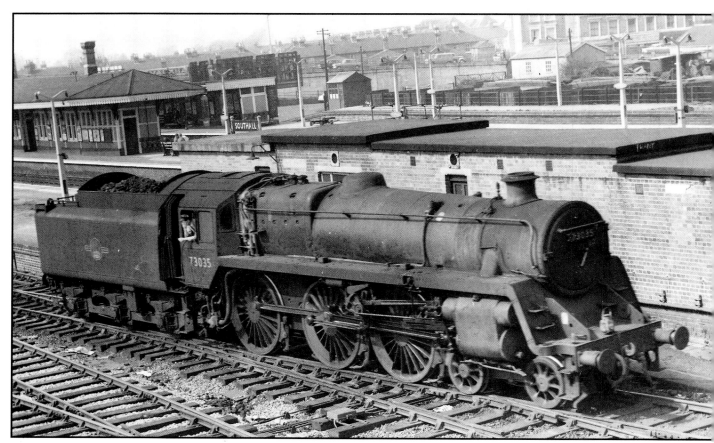

131) The fireman of BR Class 5 4-6-0 No 73035, from 6D Shrewsbury, takes things easy as his charge trundles through Southall station light engine on 3rd April 1965. Constructed at Derby Works in August 1953 and once of 84B Oxley, No 73035 had been allocated to Shrewsbury since June 1958. It departed from there in July 1965 and made the move to its last abode at 9H Patricroft in Manchester, being withdrawn in January 1968. (F.Hornby)

132) BR Class 4 4-6-0 No 75004 is sidelined at the end of a dead road at 89B Croes Newydd whilst visiting the shed from 89C Machynlleth on 9th June 1963. No 75004, one of the examples of the class to sport a double chimney, had served from 86C Cardiff (Canton), 82E Bristol Barrow Road, 82G Templecombe and 82F Bath Green Park before moving to Machynlleth in November 1962. Its final shed was at 6D Shrewsbury, being condemned in March 1967. (N.E.Preedy)

33) Its tender piled high with what appears to be little more than slack, GWR *Modified Hall* Class 4-6-0 No 7912 *Little Linford Hall* is hemmed in between two tank engines in the yard of its home depot at 84E Tyseley on 14th April 1962 shortly before being transferred to 84C Banbury after many years of erstwhile service at 84E. *Little Linford Hall* continued in service at Banbury until withdrawn in October 1965. It was cut up at Cashmores, Great Bridge. (N.E.Preedy)

34) Paired with a straight-sided tender and equipped with a double chimney (February 1961), GWR *Castle* Class 4-6-0 No 7020 *Gloucester Castle* (81A Old Oak Common) prepares to depart from Oxford station with a Paddington to Worcester express on 18th April 1964. The service from Paddington-Worcester-Hereford was one of the last to be regularly hauled by steam on the Western Region. No 7020 was taken out of service from 81C Southall in September 1964. (I.J.Hodson)

135) The GWR inspired but British Railways built Hawksworth 1500 Class 0-6-0 Pannier Tanks with their unusual appearance and outside cylinders were designed mainly for use on heavy shunting duties. No 1502 is noted out of steam in the yard of its home shed at 81E Didcot on 21st March 1954. After withdrawal in January 1961 it was sold to the National Coal Board where it continued to work until around 1970 after which it was scrapped. (A.N.H.Glover)

136) With driving wheels of only four feet one and a half inches it is remarkable that some examples of the Wolverhampton Works built GWR 2021 Class 0-6-0 Pannier Tanks were auto-fitted in earlier years, though most spent their time shunting in yards. No 2070, seen in forlorn condition outside Swindon Works on 21st September 1955 prior to being scrapped, had been a resident of 82B St.Philip's Marsh until condemned the previous month. (B.K.B.Green)

37) The 'Old Order' at Birmingham (Snow Hill) station in August 1962. 84E Tyseley based GWR *Grange* Class 4-6-0 No 6861 *Crynant Grange* clambers up the incline from Hockley and arrives with train 037, a summer holiday special to the south coast. Snow Hill station declined in importance from March 1967 until closure and dereliction in 1972. Since then a new station has risen from the ashes and the spirit of the old one has been rekindled. (N.E.Preedy)

38) GWR *Modified Hall* Class 4-6-0 No 7906 *Fron Hall*, complete with a straight-sided tender and allocated to the local shed, is on standby duty outside Reading station in case of a mainline failure on 25th July 1957. With the coming of the newfangled diesels the Reading standby locomotives were called upon quite often until the problems with the new source of motive power were ironed out. *Fron Hall* survived until March 1965, from 81F Oxford. (N.E.Preedy)

139) Eking out its last days of service, work-stained GWR 5700 Class 0-6-0PT No 4630 (82E Bristol Barrow Road) trundles up the bank towards Ashley Hill and Filton Junction from Bristol on 5th August 1965. Allocated to 88D Merthyr, No 4630 was drafted to the Southern Region in January 1959 serving at 73H Dover and 72B Salisbury before returning to the Western Region at Barrow Road in January 1964. It was withdrawn from 82E in November 1965. (T.R.Amos)

40) Allocated to 16F Burton from April to October 1964, LMS *Jubilee* Class 4-6-0 No 45721 *Impregnable* was a common sight on relief expresses between Birmingham and Bristol before moving to a final home at 8K Bank Hall. On 29th August 1964, *Impregnable* pounds towards the camera as it departs from Gloucester with a Saturdays Only relief service (1V27) to the West of England. This section of track has long been lifted and no trace remains today. (N.E.Preedy)

41) Blackened by the smoke from countless engines the large coaling stage at 82B St.Philip's Marsh overlooks the yard which hosts GWR 7200 Class 2-8-2T No 7206, a visitor to the shed from 86E Severn Tunnel Junction on 5th August 1962. Once of 86G Pontypool Road until moving to 86E in July 1959, No 7206 returned to 86G for a brief spell between January 1963 and May 1964. Its last home was at 86B Newport (Ebbw Junction) being withdrawn in July 1964. (D.K.Jones)

142) With two wooden barrows in the foreground, GWR 5700 Class 0-6-0PT No 5745, of 84E Tyseley, stands outside the entrance to Wellington shed, coded 84H, in the company of an unidentified GWR 5101 Class 2-6-2T in the late fifties. Condemned from Tyseley in November 1959, No 5745 was later noted in store at 84A Wolverhampton (Stafford Road) in January 1960. After a brief period of storage it was towed to Buttigiegs, Newport for cutting up. (R.S.Carpenter)

143) Looking almost brand new, BR Class 3 2-6-2T No 82009 is in light steam in the shed yard at 88C Barry - circa 1955. Later on in its short working life, No 82009 was allocated to 83A Newton Abbot, 84G Shrewsbury, 84H Wellington, 82A Bristol (Bath Road), 82E Bristol Barrow Road, 82B St.Philip's Marsh, 89C Machynlleth and 9H Patricroft. After withdrawal in October 1966 it was stored at 9H until being despatched to Cashmores, Great Bridge in March 1967. (D.K.Jones)

44) Conversation time on a wet and miserable looking winter's day at Worcester (Shrub Hill) station in 1960. From far off 86G Pontypool Road, February 1926 built GWR 5600 Class 0-6-2T No 5659 has been purloined by the staff at the nearby shed (85A) to carry out station pilot duties. No 5659 is standing on a centre road whilst in the process of marshalling some coaches from the *Cathedrals Express*. It was withdrawn from service in November 1965. (Tim Farebrother)

45) We complete this quartet of photographs of tank engine power with this profile of GWR 6100 Class 2-6-2T No 6108, from 81B Slough, as it rattles along in Sonning Cutting with a lengthy rake of coal empties in July 1953. In the intervening years up to being taken out of traffic in August 1965, No 6108 was based at 81A Old Oak Common, 87H Neyland, 88A Cardiff (Radyr) and 81F Oxford. It was reduced to scrap by Birds, Bynea in November 1965. (D.K.Jones)

146) An 'artist' has been at work on the bogie and buffers of GWR *Modified Hall* Class 4-6-0 No 6975 *Capesthorne Hall* which is a visitor to 84G Shrewsbury from 84B Oxley (minus shedplate) on 30th July 1960. An Oxley engine for many years, apart from a brief flirtation at 84A Wolverhampton (Stafford Road) from December 1958 to May 1959, *Capesthorne Hall* eventually took its leave of Oxley for good in September 1962, moving to 87A Neath. (D.K.Jones)

147) A busy scene at Oxford station on 30th May 1963 where GWR *Castle Class* 4-6-0 No 7002 *Devizes Castle*, of 85A Worcester, is employed on the 6.39pm express to Paddington. Occupying a centre track is sister locomotive No 5085 *Evesham Abbey*, from 82B St.Philip's Marsh. Constructed at Swindon Works in June 1946, *Devizes Castle* acquired a double chimney in July 1961. It was condemned from 85A in March 1964 after covering only 837,626 miles. (R.Picton)

48) GWR *Hall* Class 4-6-0 No 4933 *Himley Hall* (81E Didcot) leans to the curve as it sweeps past platform two at Tyseley station with a down express bound for Birmingham (Snow Hill) in 1956. Today, the buildings at Tyseley station are 'listed' and from time to time get a fresh lick of paint. There are still extensive carriage sidings here along with a diesel depot and of course the long established Birmingham Railway museum complete with a turntable. (D.K.Jones)

49) The likes of Isambard Kingdom Brunel and G.J.Churchward might well have turned in their graves at the very thought of a former London Midland & Scottish Railway Pacific penetrating into the heart of Great Western territory, but this is the case on 9th May 1964 when *Coronation* Class 4-6-2 No 46251 *City of Nottingham*, from 5A Crewe (North), visited Swindon. It is seen in the yard at 82C waiting for the return working of the 'East Midlander' special. (W.Potter)

150) The handsome breed of Somerset & Dorset Joint Railway Class 7F 2-8-0's were designed specifically for freight duties on the S & D, but in their declining years they were utilised more and more on holiday expresses, usually in a double-headed combination with other classes of locomotives. In the early sixties No 53804, based at 82F Bath Green Park, prepares to depart from Green Park station with an SLS special. It was withdrawn in February 1962. (N.E.Preedy)

151) With the winter almost at an end and the prospect of spring around the corner, GWR 7400 Class 0-6-0PT No 7404 steams and sizzles over an ashpit at its home shed at 81F Oxford in March 1962. A resident of Oxford depot for many years, No 7404 finally said goodbye to 81F in December 1963 moving westwards to South Wales and a new home at 87D Swansea East Dock. Withdrawn in June 1964 it was eventually scrapped at Birds, Morriston, Swansea. (D.K.Jones)

52) A variety of steam engines with different wheel arrangements are lined up in the shed yard at 81A Old Oak Common on a bright 26th August 1951. Included in the line-up is a GWR 4-6-0, a GWR 2800 Class 2-8-0 and GWR 4300 Class 2-6-0 No 6313 which is a visitor to Old Oak from 81F Oxford. Later in life No 6313 served from the sheds at 81C Southall and 81E Didcot. Condemned from the latter in November 1961, No 6313 was cut up at Swindon Works. (B.K.B.Green)

53) Hands in pockets a young man takes no interest in what is going on around him as he 'props' up a wall at Birmingham (Snow Hill) on 31st August 1962. Standing proudly at the head of the southbound *Cornishman* is GWR *Castle* Class 4-6-0 No 5026 Criccieth Castle, an inmate of 84A Wolverhampton (Stafford Road). On 10th September 1962 Snow Hill lost *The Cornishman* to its bitter rival at Birmingham (New Street). No 5026 survived until November 1964. (J.Schatz)

154) 'Super-power' for the 11.15am stopping train from Plymouth (North Road) to Taunton on 12th July 1956. Combining together to double-head the train at Teignmouth are GWR *Modified Hall* Class 4-6-0 No 7905 *Fowey Hall*, from 83D Laira (Plymouth), and GWR *Grange* Class 4-6-0 No 6848 *Toddington Grange*, also from Laira. *Fowey Hall* departed from 83D in November 1959, moving to 84C Banbury. It was condemned in May 1964 and cut up three months later. (F.Hornby)

155) A study of elegance and power near to Reading as GWR *Castle* Class 4-6-0 No 5007 *Rougemont Castle* (81A Old Oak Common) thunders along with an express in the summer of 1957. Introduced into traffic in June 1927, *Rougemont Castle*, late of 86C Cardiff (Canton), worked from Old Oak Common from March 1957 until February 1959. Destined to be a victim of the September 1962 slaughter programme, No 5007 was scrapped at Cashmores, Newport. (D.K.Jones)

56) A visitor from South Wales is veiled in bright sunshine as it stands in steam near to soot-encrusted buildings at 85B Gloucester (Horton Road) on 29th October 1961. The visitor, GWR 4200 Class 2-8-0T No 5246, is from 87B Duffryn Yard, a compact six-road affair once the property of the Port Talbot Railway, which closed completely on 2nd March 1964. On a visit on the 22nd of the same month the author noted thirteen locomotives in store. (N.E.Preedy)

57) Another version of the GWR 4200 Class 2-8-0 Tanks, No 4225, stands out of steam outside its home at 88J Aberdare in July 1962. Note the absence of outside steampipes as opposed to No 5246 in the previous picture. No 4225 departed from this 1908 built shed with its single covered roundhouse in September 1962 for pastures new at 87F Llanelly from whence it was withdrawn in January 1963. It was cut up at Hayes, Bridgend in December 1963. (N.E.Preedy)

158) Stabled near to the turntable at Swindon Works, BR Class 9F 2-10-0 No 92208 waits to be steamed and returned home to 88A Cardiff (Canton) on 24th June 1962 after an overhaul. Built in June 1958 and equipped with a double chimney, No 92208 was initially shedded at 83D Laira (Plymouth). By October 1963 it was no longer required by the WR authorities and was drafted to the LMR, working from the sheds at 9D Newton Heath and 12A Carlisle (Kingmoor). (N.E.Preedy)

59) With a diesel shunter in the left of the frame, GWR *Castle* Class 4-6-0 No 5020 *Trematon Castle*, an 83G Penzance steed, enters Truro station under cloudy skies with an up express bound for Paddington on 15th August 1959. Ousted from 83G in May 1960, *Trematon Castle* served briefly at 83B Taunton before moving on the following month to 83C Exeter St.Davids. Before withdrawal in November 1962 it was at 88A Cardiff (Canton) and 87F Llanelly. (Peter Hay)

60) After bringing in an up express, GWR *King* Class 4-6-0 No 6019 *King Henry V* has been released from the bufferstops at Paddington and is awaiting a path to its home shed at 81A Old Oak Common on 10th September 1957, five months after being modified with a double chimney. *King Henry V* was transferred to 86C Cardiff (Canton) in September 1960 where it remained until March 1962. Its last homes were at 84A Wolverhampton (Stafford Road) and Old Oak Common again. (B.K.B.Green)

161) The sun's rays are low in the sky as they reflect off the exterior of GWR *Grange* Class 4-6-0 No 6860 *Aberporth Grange* seen out of steam near to some piles of discarded ash in the yard at 81D Reading on 10th September 1949. In the latter years of its life, No 6860 worked from a number of sheds, these being at 83G Penzance, 87F Llanelly (twice), 83B Taunton, 83D Laira, 82B St.Philip's Marsh, 82E Bristol Barrow Road and 88A Cardiff East Dock. (D.K.Jones)

162) Three locomotives grace the yard at 83D Laira (Plymouth) on 27th June 1960. Centrepiece of this photograph is locally based GWR 4300 Class 2-6-0 No 7335 (ex. No 9313) which was allocated to 83D from June 1958 until October 1961 following a move from 82B St.Philip's Marsh. The final home for No 7335 was at 85B Gloucester (Horton Road) being condemned from there in September 1963. It was scrapped at Coopers Metals, Sharpness in May 1964. (N.E.Preedy)

63) GWR 4500 Class 2-6-2T No 5551, shedded at 83E St.Blazey, is about to clatter over pointwork with its stock, the 1.23pm local passenger train from Wadebridge as it arrives at Bodmin Road station in August 1959. This branch line was doomed to closure in 1967 along with the associated stations at Boscarne Exchange Platform, St.Lawrence Halt, Grogley Halt and Nantstallon Halt. No 5551's fate was sealed when it was withdrawn in January 1960. (Peter Hay)

64) Summer foliage hangs over the tracks at Sydney Gardens, Bath as relief express No 1M09 the 1.16pm from Bath to Nottingham passes by on 10th August 1963 hauled by GWR *Grange* Class 4-6-0 No 6838 *Goodmoor Grange*, of 86G Pontypool Road. *Goodmoor Grange* was no longer required at Pontypool Road shed by June 1964 and it moved on to 82E Bristol Barrow Road. Between then and withdrawal in November 1965, No 6838 worked from a further three sheds. (R.Picton)

165) Riddles War Department Class 8F 2-8-0 No 90466, from 81C Southall, trundles eastwards through Newport (High Street) station on 7th June 1962 with a train of steel flats shortly before being transferred to the London Midland Region at 8B Warrington. In January of the following year it moved from 8B to 26C Bolton, remaining there until September 1964 when it changed regions again, being drafted to 40E Colwick in Nottingham. (N.E.Preedy)

166) The 'Dudley Dodger' auto-train service from Dudley to Birmingham (Snow Hill) ran via Swan Village and one such train is seen leaving Soho & Winson Green station under clear signals powered by 84F Stourbridge based GWR 1400 Class 0-4-2T No 1458 in October 1956. Destined to be one of the last working examples of the class, No 1458 operated from several more sheds before being withdrawn from 85B Gloucester (Horton Road) in November 1964. (R.S.Carpenter)

57) Built by British Railways in December 1950, GWR inspired *Manor* Class 4-6-0 No 7824 *Iford Manor* (83G Penzance) stands on a through road at Totnes station with a down freight on 7th September 1955. Although we cannot tell the length of this freight from the photograph it would have been banked from Aller Junction to Totnes, probably by a GWR 5101 Class 2-6-2T. *Iford Manor* took its leave of 83G in July 1957, moving to 87G Carmarthen. (N.L.Browne)

58) A fine portrait of GWR 5101 Class 2-6-2T No 5178 seen here in steam amidst the weeds and vegetation in the shed yard at 84F Stourbridge in the West Midlands on 14th June 1953. No 5178 spent the last years of its life based at 83A Newton Abbot, being condemned from there in March 1960 and scrapped five months later at Swindon Works. The depot at Stourbridge, a single roundhouse, situated half a mile from Stourbridge Junction, closed in July 1966. (N.E.Preedy)

169) GWR 4300 Class 2-6-0 No 6327, from 82B St.Philip's Marsh, waits in an almost deserted Minehead station with the 12.20pm local passenger train to Taunton on 10th July 1957. This type of locomotive was the normal power for this line which was closed under the 'Beeching Axe' in 1971, eight years after No 6327 was withdrawn. Thankfully the line was saved by the preservation movement and today is one of the finest preserved lines in England. (F.Hornby)

170) A 'foreigner' from the Southern Region is trespassing on Western Region metals in 1954. SR Unrebuilt *West Country* Class 4-6-2 No 34004 *Yeovil*, a 72A Exmouth Junction locomotive, is caught on film near to Teignmouth with a westbound local passenger working. Constructed in July 1945, *Yeovil* was rebuilt during February 1958 at Eastleigh Works and it inhabited four more depots before being withdrawn from active service in July 1967. (D.K.Jones)

71) Paired with a straight-sided tender and based locally, GWR *Hall* Class 4-6-0 No 5989 *Cransley Hall* is in steam in the yard at 81C Southall on 10th April 1957, three months before being reallocated to 86C Cardiff (Canton). It was to move twice more during 1957, to 86E Severn Tunnel Junction and 84C Banbury. Later transfers took *Cransley Hall* to 81F Oxford and 87A Neath. It was condemmned from the latter in July 1962 and scrapped in February 1963. (N.L.Browne)

72) Divided by heaps of discarded ash which are waiting to be collected are two GWR *Castle* Class 4-6-0's Nos 7005 *Sir Edward Elgar* and 7022 *Hereford Castle* which are both in steam in the yard of their home shed at 85A Worcester on 12th July 1964. *Sir Edward Elgar*, sporting a home-made front numberplate, was built in June 1945 and renamed from *Lamphey Castle* in August 1957. It was taken out of revenue earning service from 85A in September 1964. (N.E.Preedy)

173) On most parts of the Western Region steam workings sadly came to a conclusion at the end of December 1965 and lines of dead and cold locomotives awaited their final sad journeys to the scrapyards from various depots. One such depot was 81F Oxford which became a 'dump' for many a fine engine. Standing silent at the entrance to the shed in December 1965 is GWR *Hall* Class 4-6-0 No 6944 *Fledborough Hall* stripped of names, numberplates and *dignity*. (D.K.Jones)

174) We take our leave of BRITISH RAILWAYS STEAMING ON THE WESTERN REGION - Volume five with this splendid view of BR Class 4 2-6-4T No 80043 (83G Templecombe) which has not long departed from Bath Green Park with an S & D local passenger train consisting of three coaches as it approaches Coombe Down tunnel on 6th August 1965. Once of 1E Bletchley, 73F Ashford, 73J Tonbridge and 72A Exmouth Junction, No 80043 was withdrawn in March 1966. (T.R.Amos)